A Mustard Seed

# of Faith

How hope conquered all odds

Brittney A. Paxson

Contents

This book is based on a true story and some names have been altered due to confidentiality.

Chapter 1

The Gift

In Matthew 17:20, the Bible says, "...if you have faith as small as a mustard seed, you can say to this mountain, 'Move from here to there,' and it will move. Nothing will be impossible for you." Essentially, it only takes a mustard seed of faith to move a mountain. The mustard seed is one of the strongest symbols of the Bible. It represents the ability to have paramount faith. I mean, do they know how small a mustard seed is? How can something that small move something as big as a mountain? After all, a mustard seed is only about .3 millimeters (mm). It wasn't until I was told at 18.5 weeks pregnant that my baby was diagnosed with Fetal Hydrops, a fatal diagnosis, and would not survive, that Dakota, my husband, and I had to find this "mustard seed."

I grew up in a Christian household. Growing up, my parents created the foundation for my brother and I in our faith, but I took mine by the reins when

I was graduating college. Dakota and I are from the same home town in South Florida, yet we met in college and both moved back after graduation. We got married a few years after college and were overjoyed when we found out we were expecting. I was so excited to finally be a mom. Initially, we were nervous; after all, we had just gotten married six months prior and still felt like we were kids ourselves. I had just gotten home from a work trip when Dakota told me that I was "being hormonal and should take a test." We laughed together as he was joking, but then I thought, well, it wouldn't hurt!

Dakota went to get dog food, and I went to CVS and bought pregnancy tests. I wanted to take the test alone; I didn't want to seem upset if it was negative, which I very much thought it would be. I waited two minutes for the test to show the result and there it was, bright as day with two pink lines. It was positive. I couldn't believe it. I think the words that came out of my mouth were, "there's no way!" I called Dakota to ask when he would be home, and he said he was just pulling up. I always envisioned telling him in a cute way that I was pregnant, but I couldn't wait. He walked in, saw me and immediately was in shock and didn't believe it either. We read the instructions on the box just to double-check. And yes, we were definitely pregnant! It was in that moment between the nerves and excitement that we realized how lucky and excited we were. We quickly remembered how much we had dreamt of this day, as we always knew we wanted to have children. I thanked God for this life and this baby.

When I moved home from college, I joined a bible study group through an old, high school friend and began to build my network of faith. We were all about the same age, in the same chapter of life, and were able to relate to one another. Little did I know these women would become an integral part of our story. They taught me that true friendship is one of God's greatest gifts.

As the news began to settle in, we could not contain our excitement. We told our families immediately. I was only five weeks pregnant at the time and as a first-time mom, I was not focused on the thought of something going wrong. I knew there was a chance that it may be too early to be viable, but that thought barely crossed my mind. Dakota and I went to Target and bought baby clothes that we would put in a box to share with our families. I remember being giddy because I was so eager to share the news. Our parents were thrilled; they were going to have their first grandbaby. My mom, Beth, swore she knew I was pregnant, and my mother-in-law, Rozz, screamed with excitement.

The weeks to come were full of joy and anticipation. It was hard to believe that we still had so long to go. The days were long and full of planning. Would it be a boy or a girl? What would their names be? What color should we paint the nursery? When do we order the furniture? How could we not tell everyone the news? We spent time researching all the things that new parents do. We went to baby stores, and I dreamt of the baby fitting into the clothes that Dakota would hold up. Whenever I passed by mirrors, I would touch my belly in anticipation of a baby bump.

At eight weeks pregnant, we went to our initial appointment and got to see our baby for the first time. We were brought back to the room where the tech was and she explained everything she was doing. Being able to see this little human move inside me was one of the most incredible moments. Dakota and I kept looking at each other in complete awe that this little tic tac was moving inside of me, and it was our baby. The joy was indescribable, and we couldn't wipe the smiles off our faces even if we tried.

Once we had the ultrasound in our hands, it started to sink in even more. We sent photos of us at the doctor's office to our family, and I will never forget how much joy I felt. I wanted to jump up and down in happiness. The doctor came in and said all looked good and to continue coming for the regular appointments. We left that day, dreaming of all the exciting moments to come. What name would we choose? What color of clothes would we buy? What is the best car seat? These questions flooded our minds, but we just wanted to pause and enjoy every moment. We had a baby coming. And it was ours to love forever.

The Bible says in Psalm 139:13, "For you formed my inward parts; you knitted me together in my mother's womb." What a beautiful reminder that this baby was meant for us. He or she was carefully crafted to join our family and we were chosen to be its parents, what a gift! We went to sleep that night feeling overwhelmingly grateful, anxious about the future, yet excited to finally live out all the dreams we had for a family we planned to create together.

Chapter 2

The Name

We were on our 10-week appointment, and things were going as normal. At this appointment, I got blood work done to test for Down Syndrome, Trisomy 18, and Trisomy 21, as well as test for the gender of the baby. There was no doubt we wanted to know the gender. I don't know who was more excited to find out, Dakota or me! He comes from a family of all boys, and I was hoping we would have a girl to break that cycle as Austin and Kolton, my brothers-in-law, joke and say that they "only have boys in this family."

I was nervous waiting for the results, but we were having this baby regardless of the outcome. This was the first time I had ever given blood before, and I am not a fan of needles. The process was smooth, and the nurses were great. I was glad it was over. I went on my way and knew the results would come in the next day or two.

One afternoon, I was at home and I got a call from an unknown number. I answered and it was the nurse that took my blood two days prior. She told me that she had the results and asked if I wanted to know what they were. I said, "Yes, but not the gender yet." She told me that the syndromes were negative! I was thrilled, and I remember breathing a sigh of relief, as any new mom would. I asked her to post the gender results onto the online portal so I could check it when Dakota was home, since we wanted to find out together. When he came back from work, we eagerly looked at the uploaded document on my profile, and I saw "XX chromones." In that moment, I had no recollection of what chromosomes were a boy and what was a girl, so I Googled it. It immediately clicked, and I knew we were having a girl - just what I had been praying for. I cried with happiness, and we were so thankful it would be smooth sailing from there, or at least, we thought it would be. We couldn't wait to meet her, and the days to come were full of us wondering and thinking about what she would look like.

Four of my Bible study group friends also announced they were pregnant with baby girls within a week of me finding out we were having a girl; it was a dream come true! I had this vision in my head of us four having playdates with the girls and raising our babies together, as all our babies were due within weeks of one another.

When we were in college, Dakota told me what her name would be if we ever had a baby girl. Once we knew it was a girl, we were even more excited to embark on this journey of becoming a family of three with our sweet Lily. We shared the news on Facebook, told all our friends and family, and began the reorganization of our home to make room for our new addition. Thankfully, I was feeling great. No symptoms of any kind, besides the fact that I was exhausted, I couldn't complain. At this point, I was feeling so thankful. Life was good and this baby was a blessing.

Chapter 3

The News

As I approached 18.5 weeks, we were impatiently anticipating our next appointment. We were excited to see our baby again. This appointment would be what is called the "anatomy scan." This scan is a more advanced scan that occurs when you are closer to 20 weeks. The specialist looks at all the baby's organs and body parts to ensure things are progressing as they should. Walking into this appointment, I had no idea it would be one of the worst days, if not the worst day of my life.

It was October 4th, a Monday morning, and my dad, Scott's birthday. Dakota and I had driven separately as we were going to work after the appointment. I sat in the lobby, waiting to be called back and there were other women in the waiting room with me, all of whom were expecting. I would sometimes make eye contact with one or two of them, and we would smile and connect. Even though we were complete strangers, it was like we knew what the other was feeling. Excited, anxious, and ready to see our babies on the ultrasound.

I was called in and sat on the patient's bed with Dakota next to me, holding my hand. The room was dark, and the only sources of light was from the computer screen the ultrasound tech would use and the screen we would be able to see our baby on. I think at every ultrasound check, as a mom, you are a little nervous because you just want everything to be okay. I was confident things were going well since we got the 12-week results back that she was negative for the main syndromes they tested for. The tech began, and the jelly on my stomach was a little too cold for my liking. As she hovered over my baby, we saw her in black and white. She was kicking and moving; we giggled and were ecstatic to be able to see her again. She looked like a baby on the screen this time, and we immediately felt relieved that we could see her, and she seemed ok. At our last appointment, you could not make out what the screen was showing, there was no distinct shape of a baby, but now there was. The tech did not say much but was taking photos of the baby using her machine. I later realized that ultrasound techs legally cannot say anything during an appointment if they see something wrong. The ultrasound was done and Dakota left as he had a meeting he needed to attend. Plus, with COVID-19 still relevant, they did not usually allow more than one person to talk to the doctor, so we knew he would not be allowed to stay. We felt like it would be a routine conversation and I would be on my way to work shortly thereafter.

I waited in the back for Dr. Seena, the maternal specialist, to bring me to her office. She approached me and asked, "Do you know why you are here today?" I cheerfully responded, "Yes, it was for my anatomy scan." At this point, my mind was nowhere near the thought of something being wrong; I rubbed my belly and smiled while we walked through the halls. We just saw Lily kicking and moving, plus the tests came back negative, so in our minds, we were good to go.

My world came crashing down in the following minutes to come. I follow Dr. Seena into her office, and she handed me a few pieces of paper as she looked at the images on her computer. I began to flip through them, thinking they were just formalities until I saw: Fetal Cardiogram Recommended ASAP. My brain did not register what I was reading, but then I started tearing up, and my heart was racing. I knew a cardiogram meant heart, and I asked her what was wrong. I immediately jumped to the worst conclusion but was trying to remain calm. At this point, I knew things were not okay as I thought.

Dr. Seena explained, "Something is wrong and this baby will not survive." All I heard was "something wrong...not survive." What did she just say?

"Something is wrong, and this baby will not survive." My brain couldn't compute what I heard. She continued, "the baby will either pass inside you or when she is born."

This cannot be happening. I thought I was in a bad dream. She proceeded to tell me, "the baby has fluid in her lungs and in her stomach that should not be there. The medical term for this is Fetal Hydrops. It is extremely rare, and I haven't seen it in my career much, if at all." All I heard was, "rare and haven't seen it". At this point I was in a daze. I was mentally absent and the most shocked I had ever been. Did she just tell me my baby was going to die? All I could mutter in response was "what?". There was no explanation she could give me to explain why this fluid was inside of my baby's body, but from what she told me, I knew it was a fatal diagnosis.

Dr. Seena told me this news I couldn't comprehend. I called Dakota, put the phone on speaker, and asked her to repeat everything she just said. At this point, I was heartbroken and devastated. I don't think I heard a complete sentence after she started talking again. My mind immediately assumed the worst. How could it not? The doctor told me that babies do not survive this diagnosis. She told Dakota and I that we had a decision to make about what kind of life we wanted for us and our child. I could not even begin to fathom terminating this pregnancy. Was that what she was recommending? A million thoughts ran through my mind. My baby was alive, I could feel her kicking inside of me. How could I ever do such a thing?

Dr. Seena recommended a cardiogram for the baby because if the fluid inside her was caused by a genetic issue, we would most likely see abnormalities in the heart first. I had never felt so hopeless in my life. Dakota and I were in complete shock. Dr. Seena further mentioned that IF this baby survives, we would be looking at lifelong care for her and she didn't know if the baby would make it since the amount of fluid in her body makes the "chances of survival, low". There was a less than 20% chance that babies diagnosed with this survive. There was no clarification as to why this was the situation we were in because "it can happen to anyone". Growing up, we are not taught to question doctors and at that point, I felt my life was over as I knew it. I was traumatized and all I could do was cry. I was inconsolable. How was this possible? I thought we were in the "clear"? No one tells you that something can come up during the 20-week scan. I was completely blindsided by this. In my mind, my life was over and my baby was going to die. That was what I was told, how would I know any different? I didn't even know what I could do or would do to get through this. There was no way I could handle this as the outcome. Was fate going to let this happen without a fight? I had no idea. No answers. No explanation. It made no possible sense to me.

Dakota's mind works in numbers, so he was asking for percentages and likelihoods, and Dr. Seena couldn't answer but reiterated that it didn't look promising. She mentioned that we must do an amniocentesis to better understand why the fluid was inside Lily. This is a procedure where a large needle is inserted into my belly, and a sample of cells from amniotic fluid is taken to a lab where they can dissect the microarray of all Lily's chromosomes to search for abnormalities. We could either do the test that day or go home, digest the information, and come back. The sooner the test is done, the sooner we would know if there was anything we could try to do to save Lily. We decided to get it done that day and move forward. We wanted to know what we were up against. We wanted answers. My world felt like it was moving a million miles an hour after we heard the news. It was hard to think of anything else except to do whatever we needed to do to help save Lily.

I was brought to a waiting room while they prepped for the procedure. I was not in a hospital but a normal OB office. It felt odd that this was about to happen here. Dakota was not there; he was on his way back to me from work. I called my mom and broke down. The only words I could mutter were, "something is wrong with the baby, and they don't know if she will survive." It was my dad's birthday, so I didn't want to call him then. Before we hung up, I said, "You may need to go clean out the nursery." That broke her heart.

A nurse came in and took my blood while I waited. She was kind and told me that her son was diagnosed with something rare but survived and is now a healthy five-year-old. My head was not in a place to understand this. Why was she telling me this? I was still trying to grasp what I was just told, and that alone was hard to do.

Dr. Seena was ready and called me back. It was the same ultrasound room that I was in just 30 minutes prior. She handed me a clipboard with papers on it that I must read through and sign. I was not in a place where I could do this intelligently. She told me that the papers indicated the facility is not liable for anything that goes wrong, such as a miscarriage, labor, bleeding, etc. I signed the papers, not knowing any better. I didn't care either, I wanted whatever procedure I needed to see if we could help Lily. It felt like an out-of-body experience. I felt numb. My mind was focused on one thing and one thing only: save this baby. I wish we had some hope from Dr. Seena, even if it was just a sliver. It was immediately a dire situation and the worst-case scenario, but we didn't even have any tests done or results back.

She proceeded with the amniocentesis, and the first time she went in, she did not get enough amniotic fluid, so she had to do it again. This made me uneasy. Plus, I had no numbing medicine; it was painful. I kept thinking, why would such a risky procedure have to be done again? You would think you would get it right the first time. Thankfully, the second time worked. The pain was excruciating, but I didn't care. I wanted to save our baby. I would do anything.

I had so many questions that were not answered. This doctor just told me the odds were against us, my baby will not survive, and this was a "poor prognosis". I asked her what to do about our baby shower as we were about to send out invites that week. She responded, "I would hold off on a baby shower right now." My body froze. No baby shower meant no baby. How is this happening right now? What did I do in life to deserve this? I had done so much good for others, and for what? For one of the best things in my life to be taken away from me? I felt no hope at this point. It felt like my world was turned upside down, and every dream I ever had for my baby was ripped from me for no reason other than the fact that it was a "rare condition, not normal and could happen to anyone." I felt broken. I didn't know how Dakota and I would get through this. I truly didn't even know if we could. I felt Lily moving inside of me and now, the doctor is telling me the likelihood of her surviving is slim? It didn't make any sense to me. None of it did.

When the procedure was over, Dr. Seena mentioned that there were doctors in Miami that could potentially help, Dr. Ruben Quintero and Dr. Eftichia Kontopoulos. She referred us to them and said their practice, The Fetal Institute, would call us to schedule an appointment. I didn't think much of it, and truthfully, I barely remember her mentioning this. Dr. Seena said the amniocentesis results could take up to three weeks. Three weeks of waiting to see if our baby had a chance. Three weeks of Lily moving and growing inside me before knowing if she would survive or not. How was I supposed to wait this long? It seemed unbearable.

As I waited for Dakota to pick me up after the procedure, I called my best friend, Casey. She and I have known each other since we were two years old. We've been through everything together, every chapter of life, good and bad; she is my person. She answered the phone, and I could barely speak. I managed to tell her, "Something is wrong with the baby, and we don't know if she will survive." We both start crying on the phone. She asked me for details of what was going on, but I was still trying to figure that out myself. The whole morning was a blur as I had just heard the news less than three hours ago.

Dakota picked me up, and we headed home. Immediately I got into the car, I began researching Fetal Hydrops online. Nothing good came up. Everything I read said there was no good outcome when this is diagnosed. I put my phone down and just cried. Dakota was silent, and I knew his mind was racing just as much as mine was. We got home and lay in bed all day, trying to understand what we were just told. Our world was just shattered. All we had was each other. No one else would understand this feeling. We clung to one another, and for a split second, I felt like I could get through whatever the future held because I knew I had him by my side. Dakota is a researcher. He would research something for months just to find the best option. He jumped into research on Fetal Hydrops, trying to decipher what this meant for us and Lily. As he became an expert on the topic, I was still traumatized by the news.

My in-laws stopped by to check in on us and we broke the news to them. My father-in-law, Devon, said that we should get a second opinion and find the best Fetal Hydrops doctor in the world – this was a life lesson he taught me. I was so caught up in listening and believing whatever Dr. Seena told me that I didn't second guess or question anything about it. I wish I had done that when she initially told us news about Lily. We researched all around the country and were prepared to relocate if we needed to.

I was reminded that with God, we are stronger than we think. Although, it is hard at times, we must remember that things happen for a reason, and there is a purpose for us to go through what life throws our way. God can bring us through seemingly impossible things to show us what can happen when we trust Him. A spiritual sister of mine reminded me that the truth is not what the world says it is, the diagnosis is not what you are told, you are who God says you are, the truth is what God says is the truth. That diagnosis is what God decides, no matter what the world says.

God specializes in working through us to achieve the impossible. It is easy to jump into conclusions when we don't understand something, but we must slow down and submit to His plan. In John 13:7, Jesus replied, "You don't understand what I am doing now, but soon it will be clear." Have faith that this is true.

Chapter 4

The Leap

Through Dakota's pediatrician, Dr. Ivy Faske, we were able to get an appointment the same day to see one of the best fetal cardiologists in the area, Dr. Desnet. Rozz and Dr. Ivy are friends, and Rozz immediately reached out when Dakota called her with the news. We were scheduled for a 5 p.m. appointment with Dr. Desnet that evening, so until then; we tried to relax as best as we could. This mostly entailed researching Fetal Hydrops and trying to find positive data or studies to be done, but we could not find much.

We learned that Fetal Hydrops refers to the presence of fluid in two or more places in the body. Ascites is the term for when there is fluid in the belly, and Pleural Effusion is fluid in the lungs. Lily had both. There are two types of hydrops: immune and nonimmune. Immune hydrops fetalis is a result of severe fetal anemia due to the destruction of fetal red blood cells by maternal immunoglobulin G (IgG) antibodies. Nonimmune hydrops fetalis (NIHF) is associated with numerous disorders that include cardiac, pulmonary, infectious, and genetic etiologies. NIHF accounts for almost 90 percent of hydrops cases, this was Lily's diagnosis. The incidence of NIHF ranges from 1/1500 to 1/3800. Usually, the cause of NIHF is dependent on an underlying disorder or cause.[1]

I got a phone call from a number that looked like spam, and I almost didn't answer. When I did, it was Taina, the nurse at The Fetal Institute whom Dr. Seena referred us to. Taina proceeded to tell me that they received the referral, and Dr. Quintero and Dr. Kontopoulos wanted to see me at their practice in Miami as soon as possible. We were scheduled for a 10 a.m. appointment the next morning. At least we had something to look forward to.

I texted my boss to let him know the situation. I was honest about everything with him to ensure the gravity of the situation was communicated. Thankfully, he and the rest of my team were extremely gracious and told me to take all the time I needed; I felt like that would be an eternity. Work was the last thing on my mind at this point. The evening began to roll around, and we got ready to go see Dr. Desnet. I slowly walked from the car to the building; I was still sore from the amniocenteses. It felt like I was in a dream. We checked in and waited to be called

---

1   UpToDate, http://www.uptodate.com/store, accessed January 25, 2023.

back. It was a children's hospital and they stayed late for us. I felt lucky. We saw colorful photos all over the walls, the kids area with games, and sick children lying on their mothers' laps. I couldn't help but wonder if I would ever have that with my baby. We were called in and Dr. Desnet was extremely kind. We discussed with him and he explained the diagnosis more clearly.

He told us more about Fetal Hydrops and the causes. Essentially, the fluid in her lungs and stomach could be there for a few reasons. We would not have any real answers until the amniocentesis results came back. If the fluid was caused by something in her genetics, there would be nothing we could do, and Lily would not survive. If it was caused by an infection, there would potentially be an option to take steroids to help the baby fight it off. The best-case scenario would be if the issue was caused by something structural or mechanical, meaning a blood vessel or capillary did not seal completely.

He explained that this was an extremely rare diagnosis and, again, we must wait for the amniocentesis results to determine the cause of the fluid. I was already impatiently waiting for these results and it was not even 24 hours. I knew Lily's outcome relied on these results to see what options we had, if any. Dr. Desnet told us that "there is a high probability that this baby will pass away in utero" and that "you have to be prepared for that." I broke down when he said this. It was so hard for me to hear that this baby that I wanted more than anything in the world may not survive. It was difficult to wrap my head around the news when I could feel her kicking me, and her heart beat and vitals were steady and normal. I could tell Dakota was trying to be strong for me but was holding back tears as much as I was letting them out. I couldn't believe this was our reality. Our world completely shifted in a matter of hours. It was hard to wrap our heads around the fact that this was our new normal. No answers. No hope. No idea if Lily would survive.

Dr. Desnet handed me tissues, and Dakota said, "We're sorry; we just found this out a few hours ago." Dr. Desnet looked at us in complete shock and said, "You did? You just had the amnio procedure?" I look at him through my tears and say, "Yes, we are going to do all we can to save her." He looked at us, and I could see in his eyes that he was in awe. It made me believe that we were stronger than we thought. And for a moment, I felt it.

Dr. Desnet wanted to see Lily's heart because if the fluid was caused by something genetic, usually, you would see issues in the heart first. He began the ultrasound and told us he would be honest, so I was expecting the worst. My guard was now up, and I was still disoriented, trying to understand all the information we were given that morning. It felt like life was moving as fast as a bullet train, and I was a passenger holding on for dear life with no control over the outcome. He was silent while doing the ultrasound. What felt like an hour went by, and he looked up and told us that things are looking good, and Lily's heart is operating normally. I let out a sigh of relief and tears of happiness. A few hours ago, I was told she would not live. And now, I am hearing that she has all four chambers of her heart, and this doctor was pleased with what he saw. For a millisecond, we saw a glimmer of hope.

Dr. Desnet gave us his business card after we told him we were going to Miami the next day to see Dr. Quintero and Dr. Kontopoulos. On the back of the card, he wrote "normal cardio function." He mentioned that he has previously worked with these doctors and they performed miraculous procedures on babies and unborn babies. He said we would be in the right hands, so I could not help but feel like we might have a chance. I decided that in that moment, I was not going to give up hope. Lily needed her mommy, of all people, to stay strong and believe in her and believe that she would make it.

There was nothing we wouldn't do. No amount of money or time we wouldn't spend give to help save our baby. We left the appointment with Dr. Desnet feeling glad that her heart was normal but worried about what the test results would come back as since that would determine everything. That night, we continued researching the best doctors for this condition all over the country. Between the tears and anxiety that filled the house, we hugged, and I prayed we would get through this and that Lily would get through it. I prayed for it to be a bad dream and that it would be all over when I woke up, and she would be fine. But that wasn't God's plan for us. Before we slept that night, Dakota looked at me and said, "If it's not genetic, we'll bring our girl home." That was our goal, to bring her home.

I tried to make myself fall asleep, but my mind was racing. For one of the first times in my life, I felt paralyzed. There was nothing we could do. We had no control over any part of this situation, at least at that moment, I didn't think I did. Then it hit me. God was my answer. I didn't know how this situation could turn into something good, but all I had to cling to was my faith. That was the only thing I could hold onto. I was totally and completely out of control. I knew I needed to pray harder and deeper than I ever had. And that was what I did. I asked Dakota to pray with me over Lily, something that seemed new to us. From that night on, we prayed over our baby together every night.

Chapter 5

The Doctors

The next morning, we headed to Dr. Quintero and Dr. Kontopoulos in Miami. Unsure of what would happen and mostly wanting answers, the two-hour drive was daunting. My mind was racing, and I was thinking of all the scenarios we could end up in. What if they couldn't help? What if they don't know what to do about this condition? Twenty-four hours ago, we received the worst news of our life. We were not sure how this appointment would turn out, but we had to keep the hope that these specialists would know what to do.

We arrived in the waiting room, and there were pictures of babies on canvases all over the office walls; these were the babies that these doctors saved. They were the most precious things, and I thought to myself, if Lily makes it, I would give them a canvas with her photo on it too. Dr. Kontopoulos saw us first, and she was kind to us. She could tell we were coming off little sleep and 24 hours of tears, fears, and worries. She did an ultrasound and confirmed that there was fluid in Lily's lungs and stomach that shouldn't be there. She told us that we were in the right place; they had seen this before and helped babies with similar conditions. I was asking questions through my tears, and she drew pictures for us to better understand the situation. I knew immediately that this was the right place to be, I could sense it. Dr. Kontopoulos had this aura about her that exemplified compassion and a motherly touch.

It got to a moment where I couldn't control my emotions and she held my hand. She reassured me that they will do all they can to save our baby, and I immediately felt an ounce of hope. Dr. Quintero came in and stood with his arms crossed in front of him, wearing his lab coat. He mentioned that "it does not look good." He also said, "We should be thankful we caught the fluid now and saw it this early in the pregnancy." He reiterated that we must wait for the amniocentesis results, which I expected.

Both doctors reviewed the ultrasounds and confirmed that Lily's heart looked normal, and her lungs are not compromised by the fluid. The best-case scenario is that the cause of the fluid is a mechanical or structural cause, and we are candidates for a thoracoamniotic shunt surgery. If we qualified, the surgery would be done laparoscopically, where they place a shunt through me into the baby's chest cavity to help drain the fluid. The worst case is that if the cause is genetic, there is likely nothing we can do, and no matter how many times we try to remove the fluid, it would keep coming back, and she wouldn't survive. We left the appointment assured that these were the right doctors to be with. It seemed like they were confident in their abilities and truly cared about helping us bring our girl home. They wanted us to come for a check-up every week and I thanked God we were now in these doctors' hands.

Dakota works from home already, and my manager kindly allowed me to do so as well. The last thing I wanted was for my co-workers to see my belly and talk about the baby. I wasn't sure how I would hold up in such a public setting like that. We spent a lot of time outside on our porch and with family, discussing the status of the pregnancy and the news we heard from all the doctors.

We had to remember that no matter the situation one passes through in life, there is a reason or purpose that God allows such things to happen to us. He said in His word that even in those hard times, He will be with us and would never allow the challenges to triumph over us, but through those challenges, His name will be made manifest. We had to trust and believe that He was with us every step of the way, guiding our steps and guarding our hearts, that was all we had to hold onto.

Chapter 6

The Support

A few days later, we received a call and found out that Lily was negative for a viral infection. Dr. Seena was the one who gave me the news, and she mentioned that she was surprised to hear this as she thought the cause was an infection. This crossed infection off the list. I felt glad but also nervous because now, we were left with what we considered the best-case scenario and the worst-case scenario. We knew the fight was not over, as we are still waiting for the rest of the genetic test results to come back. This took time since the test looked at the microarray of all 23 pairs of chromosomes. The cause of the fluid could be life-threatening based on genetic results, or it could be something that we can try to fix, such as the shunt surgery to help drain the fluid. My prayer continued to be for the cause of the fluid to be something we could do something about. The following week, we went back to The Fetal Institute, and Dr. Quintero explained that her left lung had gotten better since the last time we were there, but her right lung got a little worse. He explained that surgery wasn't the end all be all, and he didn't want to have to intervene if he didn't have to, as the surgery comes with its own risks as well. Puncturing the uterus is never something you want to do. He told us that her feet were normal, her heart was not in overdrive, and her lungs were currently getting oxygen, which were all the things that potentially wouldn't be the case if it was a genetic issue. We needed this good news in the midst of waiting. I prayed and thanked God for this bit of good news.

Romans 8:18 says, "For I consider that the sufferings of this present time are not worth comparing with the glory that is to be revealed to us." Essentially it is saying that the pain you've been feeling can't compare to the joy that is coming. I couldn't imagine how much joy would have to come that could compare to the pain I was feeling. I felt like I was in a nightmare. A bad dream. It was hard to keep the faith, but it was all I had.

The days were long, waiting for the phone call with the results. We tried to have hope, but it was tough. I remembered that all we needed was a mustard seed of faith, so I clung to this thought. All I needed was .3mm of faith, and this mountain should move, right? We prayed like we had never prayed before. I was on my knees every morning and night, praying for a miracle. I came to accept the fact that this was the situation we were in, and I was going to channel all my energy into giving this to God. I continuously prayed for Him and the Holy Spirit to work in our lives. I prayed for Dakota and me to have the strength to get through whatever His plan was, even if it was not what we wanted. I had to come to terms with the fact that if God's plan was opposite of ours, we would be okay because that was His plan all along. I prayed that He would give Lily the strength to keep fighting; I wanted her to be here more than anything. I knew that one day, I would understand why we were going through this, and I knew that there was a bigger purpose out of my control. Even in the lowest moments, I knew that God had a purpose for us, and more importantly, He had a purpose for Lily.

Every morning, I would make my French Vanilla decaf coffee and sit on our porch, read devotions, and listen to worship music. This became my ritual, my haven. I would sometimes do this for 10 minutes and sometimes, two hours, depending on the day. I felt like this was my time to reflect on everything and be alone with Lily and my feelings. I would cry out of sadness and worry, and other times, I would cry out of happiness for having a God to put my hope in.

The support that began to form around us was breathtaking. Our family and friends truly created a community of prayer and hope around Dakota, Lily, and me.

The love, care, and support that we felt was nothing like I had ever seen or felt before. My mom had a friend group praying for us; Rozz had friends praying for us, all our aunts and uncles, cousins, our brothers, my dad, Devon, coworkers that we were close with, as well as all our friends from college, the list goes on. My Bible study girls became my prayer warriors, and I updated them on every appointment. They would text me every Wednesday because they knew that was when we went to Miami and gave me the much-needed words of encouragement. I leaned on them often and was thankful to have them in my life. As time went on, my dreams of us having playdates with our girls slowly seemed to slip farther away, but I kept the faith, even when the odds were against us.

One morning, I was in Rozz and Devon's backyard. They live close by, on the intracoastal, and I wanted to get away from our house and just have a moment to breathe. I was alone with my thoughts and my worship music, and my heart began to ache. I was in a place of complete and utter sadness. I was going to lose the baby. I truly thought that was our outcome. I tried to keep the faith and stay positive, but it took all my energy every day to do this, and it was harder some days than others. It began to wear on me. Rozz came outside and sat at my feet. She talked to me and told me to name my fears. I told her that my biggest fear was Lily not surviving. I was afraid to lose her, and I was afraid if that happened, I wouldn't be able to recover. She told me, "God has a purpose, and although we cannot see it, there IS a reason this is happening." God can use us during times of trial to show us what is possible when we have faith. We may never know why things happen, but that is something we must believe because it is all we have. Putting your life in God's hands during the light times in life is easy but putting your life in His hands in the dark times, now that is faith.

Once we cried and talked, I felt better. I needed that. I needed a reminder to keep fighting. Lily needed me to fight for her. I prayed over my belly that she wouldn't give up and would stay strong. Now, it was my turn to stay strong and keep fighting. Every shower I took, I would talk to her and tell her specifically what was going on and tell her she needed to keep fighting and not give up. I'll never forget those vulnerable moments that only Lily and I went through.

Throughout this journey, our brothers were checking in, praying for us, and ensuring we were okay. This was their niece, after all. My brother, Ben, and Dakota's two brothers, Austin and Kolton, are close. I love that we all have the relationship that we do. On the night of our wedding, all three of them wore "Brother Out-Law" t-shirts. They are three of the most caring and loving men I know. Having a sibling is such a special bond; there is no one that gets you like your siblings do.

Kolton attends the University of Notre Dame, where Austin attended and where Rozz is very involved. Kolton's dorm held special masses dedicated to Lily where 30 to 50 people would gather and pray for us. Rozz gathered her friends at the University, and there were people that prayed for Lily every single day. Those moments of people coming together that did not even know us were beyond incredible and touched my heart in so many ways. The community and power of prayer is so strong.

Matthew 21:22 says, "and whatever you ask in prayer, you will receive if you have faith." And Mark 9:29 says, "this kind cannot be driven out by anything but prayer." I could see this working in our lives and in our hearts, and I knew praying was all we had. There is beauty in surrendering to Jesus, and there's nothing stronger than the body and community of believers working together in prayer. Throughout my pregnancy, during every online church service I attended, I would submit a prayer request for Lily and continue to ask for our baby to be healed. I wanted her so desperately.

Chapter 7

The Genetics

One morning, I got a phone call that the nursery furniture was ready to be delivered. I broke down. It was November, and the furniture wasn't supposed to be delivered until January. How was I supposed to set up her nursery when we didn't even know if she would survive? I felt torn. So many thoughts ran through my mind. Do we cancel the order? Do we store it in a storage unit? Do we have it delivered and risk having to get rid of it at some point? I called Dakota as I was crying and told him about the delivery call. We talked and he told me to have it delivered. Until we heard otherwise, we were going to keep fighting and stay positive that things would be okay.

I felt like this was a cruel joke that the universe was playing on me. It was on days like this that the devil crept into my mind to try and tear down the armor of God I had been building. I shoved those negative thoughts to the side and prayed that God continued to have us in His hands. Proverbs 16:9 says, "We can make our plans, but the Lord determines our steps." I had to trust that there was a purpose for all the pain and suffering. The furniture arrived, and it was beautiful. It was a light-finished grey color. Once the movers left, I broke down crying in the nursery. The emotions were overwhelming. Seeing the crib placed in the room where I wasn't even sure my baby would come home to was mentally and emotionally heart-wrenching. I sat on the floor, leaning on the crib, praying with every bone in my body. My heart ached, and I craved for this baby to be okay. I was so sad, and angry that this was our situation, and it was hard to be hopeful since we hadn't heard about the amniocentesis results yet.

Four hours later, I received a call from an unfamiliar number when Rozz was at our house, and Dakota was with Devon. The number left a voicemail. I knew it had to be the doctor giving us the results of the amniocentesis. I ran over to my in-laws, and Devon and Rozz waited outside for Dakota and me to finish listening to the voicemail. I wasn't sure if this was Dr. Seena with the results, but I had a feeling it was. I remember signing a paper allowing the results to be shared via voicemail.

Dakota and I held each other as we opened the voicemail and listened to it. The second I heard the words, "the baby's genetics are normal; there are no chromosome abnormalities." I lost control of my legs and fell to the ground. I was crying and thanking God continuously. I couldn't catch my breath. I was in utter disbelief. I was thinking the worst up until now to guard my heart and prepare myself. The emotions and feelings were overwhelming, to say the least. Dakota and I couldn't stop hugging and crying. It felt like the timing of the phone call was a wink from God saying, "See what happens when you trust Me." We accepted the furniture delivery and trusted His plan, then we found out we had a fighting chance. We had already been through and done so much; we weren't even close to being finished fighting for our girl. We knew, at this point, we could do something to save her, or at least try to. The fight wasn't over; it was just beginning.

Jesus is THE miracle worker, and this was the start of a journey we couldn't have fathomed possible, even if we tried. We prayed for the cause of the fluid to be something we could do something about, and our prayer was answered. We may have chance to bring our girl home.

We went back to Miami a day later, and Dr. Quintero told us that Lily's left lung had healed on its own and the fluid in her belly also went away. I was shocked. I asked Dr. Quintero to double-check and triple-check again after that. This never happens on its own; what a miracle. Even he was surprised. He couldn't believe that it healed on its own. It was at this moment that I truly felt that Jesus had His hand on our baby. In the eye of the storm, He made it clear we had to trust Him. He showed us what trusting Him can do. Miracles are possible.

As Dr. Quintero was doing the ultrasound, he also saw that Lily's right lung got better but still needed some help. I qualified for surgery, and it was scheduled for the following day. Not only was I afraid for Lily, but my biggest fear was needles, and I was about to have a giant one stuck into my pregnant belly and then into my unborn baby. Medicine is fascinating. I still couldn't believe that the technology exists for this to be able to happen. I sure am thankful for it, though.

I would be 22 weeks along for this surgery. I felt overwhelmed at the thought of having surgery and trusting a doctor to perform this procedure on me and Lily. It was terrifying, but I trusted God and didn't question it. I knew He placed these doctors in our lives for a reason. Lily didn't have a middle name yet, let alone was born yet, but she was about to have surgery that would hopefully save her life. We had to do whatever it was that could help her. This was our only option to potentially save her. What a miracle to have this opportunity. Not to mention we only needed to help one lung now, her right one.

The night before the surgery, Dakota and I were in the kitchen. We were quiet but aware of how the other was feeling. I had bags packed as I knew we would stay overnight after the procedure. We were unsure what the next day would bring, and all I could think about was the fight that we had in front of us. We were fighting to save our baby, and it was a long road ahead. I looked at him and said, "if anything happens tomorrow, save her, not me-" He cut me off midsentence and I knew it was because he didn't want to think about that. But if what it took to save our baby was something happening to me, I was willing to take that risk. She was our everything. All we wanted was to bring her into this world. I had never felt this kind of love in my life. As any mother, I would do anything for her.

 The next day, Dakota and I were in the nursery before we headed to the hospital. We stood over the crib, held the railings and each other. I remember being so scared that I got emotional and prayed out loud. I prayed for the hands of Dr. Quintero to do the right thing, for him to have the knowledge and ability to make the right calls and be successful in his efforts. I prayed for Lily to survive the surgery, stay strong, and for my body to provide her with whatever she needed. After all, this was a risky procedure.

 The anxiety that encompassed us on the way to the hospital was crushing. I started to read Bible verses to help calm my nerves and I came across Matthew 6:25-29. Jesus tells us not to be anxious about things in life, like what we will eat or drink, and poses the question, can you gain a single hour to the span of life by being anxious? Reading this reminded me that it does no good to put my energy into worrying about something I could not control the outcome of. The verse continues and says, "and why are you anxious about something like clothing? Consider the lilies of the field, how they grow: they neither toil nor spin." I smiled when I read this. Some say that lilies represent rebirth and hope; I like to think that too. If Jesus takes care of the lilies in the field, He will certainly take care of me and my Lily. What a beautiful reminder of His love for us. The verse concludes by saying, "therefore do not be anxious about tomorrow, for tomorrow will be anxious for itself." After reading this, I was ready for the unknown, the surgery; ready to conquer this step in our journey to try and save our baby.

Chapter 8

The Surgery

We arrived at the hospital and I felt petrified with fear. I was not sure how I would be able to wrap my head around what I was about to do. I had never even had an IV before. I prayed for the Holy Spirit to overwhelm me with comfort and peace. I listened to worship music for the entire time prior to going into the operating room (OR). Dakota and I prayed over Lily and held hands, reassuring each other that we could get through this.

We were admitted into the room, and a nurse named Val came in to do the IV. She was the happiest person I think I have ever met. She was amazing and known on that floor for being the best at IVs. I was so thankful for that! Our room was in the maternity ward, and we were waiting for someone to come in and tell us what to expect. A few hours went by, and we heard a baby cry. Dakota looked at me and says, "that baby was just born." I tear up as I hope that could be us one day. As I held my belly and felt Lily kicking, I couldn't wrap my head around that not being an option for us. The nurses eventually came, and I did not know what to expect as this was my first major surgery. Thankfully, they explained what was going to happen and helped me on a gurney. They wheeled me into the hallway and I hugged Dakota and said I will be back soon. I couldn't imagine what that must have been like, watching me get wheeled away and just having to wait there. He was being so strong for me.

As we got off the elevator on the first floor, it was a bit of a shock. It smelt like pure alcohol, and the lights were as bright as what I would envision an interrogation room would be. We wheeled past other patients; some were unconscious since we were in the ER area. I closed my eyes as that scared me. We got a bit further down, and I felt like I was in a real-life Grey's Anatomy scene, just waiting for other doctors to rush past us and scream they needed backup. We get into OR #7, and there are more monitors and machines than I have ever seen in one place. There were wires and monitors hanging from the ceiling, bright lights shining down on the OR table, the smell of iodine, and about 10 different people getting the room ready.

There was an anesthesiologist named Linda. She was around her mid-50s and had an inviting voice. I told her I was scared and she held my hand through all the prep that was being done. She was such a kind human. Another nurse named Annie was painting iodine on my belly and then proceeded with the catheter. Linda put my cap on and hung the drape. Annie strapped my arms down. I asked Linda if it would hurt, and she said it wouldn't since I would be getting anesthesia. The real reason I would get that is so that Lily would relax and not move a lot during the surgery; I just got to reap the benefits of having the drug in me.

During the surgery, Dr. Quintero was going to place a shunt into the right side of Lily's chest cavity to help drain the fluid. I could hear the team next to me discussing the game plan. The surgery would be done laparoscopically, guided by an ultrasound. This meant, while I was awake, Dr. Quintero would insert a long needle through my belly and into Lily's body, where he injected the thoracoamniotic shunt into her chest cavity. The shunt would help pull the fluid out and stay in her until she was born, but it had a 50% chance that it would fall out.

As Dr. Quintero began the surgery, I felt relaxed but still a bit anxious. Linda began stroking my hair and played instrumental relaxation music on her phone for me, which helped calm my nerves. He gave me localized numbing medication, and I felt a pinch. After that, I didn't feel a thing. I had to be completely still because he was going in with the needle, and the last thing that needed to happen was the needle hitting something like Lily's spine. The entire procedure took about seven minutes. He was in and out. He had to be. There was only a short window where this would work and Lily would be in a standstill place for a long duration. I couldn't believe how quick it was. I cried with happiness when it was over, thanking God for this chance to hopefully save Lily.

Dr. Quintero came over behind the drape to talk to me. He held my hand and smiled, and said I did a great job, and that the surgery went perfectly. He had seen some fluid already leave Lily's lung the second the shunt was inserted. It couldn't have gone better, he said. I just kept thanking him over and over.

After I was cleaned up, I was brought back to our room and was eager to see Dakota. Dr. Quintero was there, giving him the details and good news of how it went. Dakota smiled when he saw me, and I was so glad to see him. I felt relieved. Dr. Quintero told us that the way he put in the shunt should help. He described what he did, and I had no clue what he meant, but I trusted he did the right thing. We called our parents and gave them the news. They were so happy to hear from us. My mom Face-timed me immediately. She was so overjoyed. I was her baby and I was doing something to save my baby. I can't imagine how that felt for her. From the beginning, my mom was convinced that Lily just needed time. She told me every day since we had received the news that "Lily just needs time to grow," "give her time," etc. Turned out she was right because it was now a waiting game. We had to wait for her lungs to grow and hoped that the fluid wouldn't be in the way for them to do so. I stayed in the hospital overnight, and we ordered Chick-Fil-A for dinner, my favorite meal, including a milkshake, of course. After my discharge, we would head to Dr. Quintero and Dr. Kontopoulos to get an ultrasound and see how the shunt was holding up.

The next day, we met with Dr. Quintero and he was pleased with the surgery and the shunt placement. He said the shunt was in the perfect place, and Lily was in the perfect position for the surgery to be done, almost like she knew to be facing a certain way and was saying, "here you go, here's my side." When we got an ultrasound the day before surgery, Lily was not in a position where the surgery would be possible. God is so good. We saw that the fluid in the right lung decreased by about 20%, but we had to keep praying that the shunt stayed in and her right lung bounced back. Up until this point, her lung was like a squished balloon due to the fluid, so we needed it to expand and grow. We left the appointment feeling hopeful. We prayed for the cause of the fluid to be something we could do something about and this seemed to be the case.

Chapter 9

The Opportunity

We went to Dr. Quintero and Dr. Kontopoulos in Miami every Wednesday to get monitored and have ultrasounds done. Throughout the rest of the pregnancy, since we had received the news, I had my guard up. It was difficult to be excited again, but I knew that we had God on our side. We were in a dark tunnel, with no indication of light on the other side, but God was holding our hand through this journey.

One week after the surgery, we drove to see Dr. Quintero; this also happened to be my birthday. Before our appointment, we had some time to kill, so we went to La Esquina Del Lechon for a Cuban sandwich, which became a routine every time we went down south. Dakota's uncle, Victor, owns the restaurant, and some other family members work there. We would update them on our weekly appointments, and even the staff were praying for us.

The community of support around us seemed to be growing every week.

After lunch, we went to Victor's family's Catholic store. I am not Catholic, but I have learned more about the religion and appreciate it. We saw a few things and I picked out a necklace with a cross on it, a stuffed animal, and the Prayer Lamb. I wore the necklace almost every day and planned to put the lamb in Lily's nursery. I was trying to stay positive and ignore the fact that this may not work out the way I wanted. I had to keep my faith and hope alive - Lily needed me to do that for her while she was also fighting herself. I was eager to see her on the ultrasound again and receive an update on how great the surgery worked.

Dr. Quintero was quiet at the start of our appointment and I was afraid something was wrong. He told us that her right lung hadn't expanded as much as he would have liked and even expected. He said it was hard for him to understand why this was the case. He didn't have an answer. This was defeating and not the news I wanted, especially on my birthday. He wanted to give Lily one more week to see if her lung expanded and the fluid drained more. If the right lung hadn't changed, we would have a second surgery to place another shunt in Lily's chest cavity. Dr. Quintero explained to us that we were under a ticking time clock. The lungs are a unique organ, and when they do not get something they need, such as blood flow or oxygen, they begin to shut off and stop fighting to survive. We had to help Lily's lungs as much as we could before they got to this point.

I left the appointment feeling overwhelmed and upset that the surgery didn't work like it was supposed to. What if the second surgery didn't work? I did not even think it was an option for the first surgery not to work. I was confused and overwhelmed. It felt like one thing after another, and just when you think you see the light at the end of the tunnel, a rock falls, and you're stuck in the tunnel with no way out again. But despite the odds being against us, I kept reminding myself that I prayed for this. I had to. I prayed for the cause of the fluid to be something we could do something about. God answered my prayer and that was something to be thankful for.

We got home and initially planned to go to a nice steak dinner for my birthday. I didn't want to go and thought it would be best to cancel and just stay home. I wasn't in a celebratory mood. Dakota told me it would be good to get out of the house, so we went. I didn't feel like being there, and had to hold back tears a few times, but I was glad we got some time to talk and be together. Overall, it was nice, and we talked about all our dreams and plans for life when we got to bring Lily home. We had to stay positive.

That night while reading *In a Pit with a Lion on a Snowy Day*[2] by Mark Batterson, I remembered God is in the business of strategically placing us in the right place at the right time. It was hard to believe this at that moment, but we had to keep the faith.

It was at this time that I had to have faith that God was ordering our footsteps and was going to help us through this. I went to sleep that night, remembering that sometimes, the biggest problems present the greatest opportunities for God to reveal His glory and His purpose. I hoped this could be one of those opportunities.

---

2   *Batterson, Mark. In a Pit with a Lion on a Snowy Day: How to Survive and Thrive When Opportunity Roars, Multnomah, New York, 2016, accessed February 5, 2023.*

Chapter 10

The Foundation

The following week at Dr. Quintero's office, he decided we needed another surgery as soon as possible. The fluid had not gone down enough to make a good enough impact on her lung growth, and we had no time to waste. I was set up for surgery the following day. We got home, packed our bags, and rested before enduring another journey in the morning.

After barely sleeping, we prayed over Lily's crib before heading to the hospital the next day. This time I prayed that the surgery would work. I prayed for strength for my body to get through this, but mostly, I prayed for Lily's strength. We needed her to keep fighting. I would be 25 weeks during this surgery, technically a viable pregnancy at this stage, but with us, that was not the case. When we got to the hospital, I was required to sign more papers this time around.

Since I was 25 weeks, if anything was to happen during the surgery that was harmful to the survival of the mother, the baby would be taken via cesarean delivery to save the mother and the child. I was nervous and worried the surgery wouldn't work, just like it didn't the first time. But I knew it was out of my hands. We arrived at the hospital, and since we had done this before, I knew what to expect.

The nurses came and took my vitals, and I was calmer than before. I saw Val and feel a bit of comfort and familiarity. I was praying and thanking God for the opportunity to do something to save our baby. We kept reminding ourselves that this was what we prayed for. We prayed for the cause of the fluid to be something we could do something about.

We were in a different room but still felt more relaxed than when we were there the first time. The nurses came in, and I was listening to my worship music on my headphones. I did this to get into the "zone." If there is even a "zone" to get into for this type of thing. I waved goodbye to Dakota as the nurses came and wheeled me down to the first floor of the hospital. Again, I smelled the alcohol and pictured myself in Grey's Anatomy, but in this scene, there was no emergency, just some patients going by and nurses waving hello. I got to the OR, and lay on the table to get prepped. Linda wasn't there this time, but her counterpart, Leah, was there. I felt calm at this point like I was in the right hands. Annie wasn't there, but Sasha was, another kind doctor.

She was prepping the iodine and the catheter. I knew this process all too well. I felt the anesthesia kick in. I knew what to expect from here, so I tried to relax. I can hear Dr. Quintero and Dr. Kontopoulos talking quietly with their team. At this point, I knew something was going on. They hadn't started the surgery, but the ultrasound tech was still looking at my belly.

After a few minutes, Dr. Quintero told me that the surgery was too risky to do at that point, and they called it off. Lily wasn't in the right position. I was overcome with disappointment. What happens now? I thought time was of the essence. I was glad they didn't risk it, but now, what do we do? I was left with a lot of questions. I was brought back to the room and Dakota was confused as to why I was back so early. I began to cry. The first surgery didn't work. The second wasn't possible. It felt like we were running out of options. We were discharged after I recovered from the anesthesia. We tried to wrap our heads around what options we had, but it was unclear. All we knew is Dr. Quintero was our only hope.

The next morning, we headed to Miami and Dr. Quintero made the decision that the third attempt and second shunt placement would be scheduled for three days later. We were getting down to the wire and needed to place another shunt into Lily as the fluid wasn't going down and was now becoming detrimental to her lung growth. We could feel the urgency from him and Dr. Kontopoulos as they were discussing the next steps with us. We knew this was the only way we had a chance at Lily making it.

Dr. Quintero began to talk to us about this foundation called the Brianna Marie Foundation. In that moment, I couldn't recall exactly why he was telling us, but I tried to listen as best as possible after being upset that the second surgery didn't work. He proceeded to explain that a baby named Brianna Marie passed away from Fetal Hydrops. The mother, Aran, and her husband, Patrick, already had two boys and were excited for their little girl, but she couldn't grow in time to survive. Aran and Patrick traveled all over the U.S. to fight for Brianna and underwent numerous shunt surgeries, as well as experimental surgeries, but they were too late. Had they seen Dr. Quintero and Kontopoulos only five weeks earlier, they may have saved their baby. As I was looking at the foundation website, my heart ached for this family. This could be us. We could potentially suffer the same loss as Aran and Patrick did.

Why was Dr. Quintero mentioning this? I was worried he thought our situation would end up the same. I had to put that aside and keep the hope alive. Keep the faith that we made it in time and Lily would be healed. We headed home after the appointment, and Dakota and I were feeling more nervous than before. We were getting to a point where we needed this fluid to be removed, or else her lung would not grow enough in time for her to breathe on her own, let alone survive.

It was on the drive home that I read a quote that motivated me just when I needed it most. It said, "Be so confident in God's plan that you don't even get disappointed anymore when things don't go your way." This stuck with me because things weren't going my way. The attempt to save my baby didn't work. And now, I wasn't sure what was going to happen. I could feel myself getting more anxious as time went on because I knew we needed a solution and fast if Lily had a fighting chance. I knew she needed me to stay strong, especially in moments when I felt like the walls were too tall to conquer. I told myself I was going to be confident in God's plan, whatever it was, and trust He knew what was best.

Sometimes, it's hard to see God working in the middle of a storm or in the middle of our story. Whenever you seem to be in this place, you want to trust His heart but you can't seem to trace His hand. Let Lily be a reminder that He's not done. What may seem like God's inactivity is never His incapability. He is working things for our good. He is able.

Chapter 11

The Sign

It was the day of the third surgery attempt and we headed to the hospital. By now, I knew exactly what to pack and what I would need. I was admitted to the hospital in the morning and felt more uneasy than the past two times I was there. I was praying a lot and hoping God would give me a sign to relax and trust Him. I knew there was hope in the unknown, and I knew I wasn't supposed to ask God for "signs," but I think He knew in my heart that it was something I could use after the past two surgeries hadn't been as successful as hoped. I had so many fears, but at this point, I was fearful the surgery wouldn't work or be able to happen again. I was fearful that Lily would not be in the right position. I was fearful that God's plan was the opposite of what I had hoped for. I was fearful she wouldn't be okay or even make it. I had to remember there was a purpose in the pain and a plan that was larger than I could ever imagine. I had to believe there was a reason; it was the only thing that got me through.

The nurse came in to take me down to the OR. I could only imagine how scary this was for Dakota, seeing his pregnant wife being wheeled away without having any ability to help me or his baby. The nurse asked me questions and I noticed that she was one of the most beautiful women I had ever seen, almost angelic looking. Her hair was dark, and her skin was smooth; she was radiating, or at least it seemed like it to me. I peeked at her name tag, and read her name, "Faith." I giggled a little and in that moment, I knew I didn't have to worry. God had it all under control. This nurse was my sign. I told her that I thought she was meant to be there and she smiled and started tearing up. I texted our family group chat and they couldn't believe "Faith" was her name either. It didn't seem like a coincidence. God had me in His arms, Lily in His hands, and Dakota by His side. It felt like Faith literally and figuratively wheeled me to the OR that day.

We got to the OR, and I recognized some familiar faces. The procedure didn't seem so intimidating anymore. Linda was there as the anesthesiologist and I was glad to see her. Faith was there prepping me and told me she would be right by my side the whole time. I still wished I didn't have to be back. Dr. Quintero huddled the team and went over the plan for the procedure. He began and I was nervous that this attempt won't work, but then I remember my "sign." Faith was there. He gave me the numbing shot and inserted the long needle into my belly. As he inserted another shunt into Lily's chest cavity, the ultrasound tech guided him, just as she did for the previous surgery. Again, seven minutes total was all it took to hopefully save Lily's life. Dr. Quintero finished and said that it was textbook surgery, as good as it could be. I was so thrilled. We had another chance. I couldn't wait to see Dakota. We were hopefully going to bring our girl home. As I was getting cleaned up, I asked Dr. Quintero to go tell Dakota how it went. I was thanking him continuously. This man could have just saved my daughter's life. What a hero.

The wave of relief that I felt took over my emotions. Sometimes, it's hard to remember all we went through to get here because we were so focused on the individual moments and just trying to get by. We felt like we were helping Lily and giving her the means to fight. That was what we were supposed to do as parents, right? We exhausted all options to do so. We stayed strong for her and conquered so many fears along the way.

After the surgery, I got wheeled back to the room, and Dakota talked to Dr. Quintero. He reiterated that all went well, he placed the shunt in a specific way, and was extremely pleased with how it went. Now, we just must give her time and see what happens. Patience was never my strong suit, but now more than ever, I needed to find it. We needed her right lung to grow. But we had to give her time. Just like my mom had been telling me.

One of my favorite Bible verses is Proverbs 3:5-6 which says, "Trust in the Lord with all your heart and lean not on your own understanding." This was what I had to do; this was what I lived by. I had to trust God's plan for us; my faith in this was all I had and could hold onto. As I was recovering, a notification popped up on my phone from the Bible app I have. It was that day's daily motivation message. It said, "God is saying to you today: Trust Me. I've stayed with you through every storm in your life. I've given you all that you need. I have and always will protect you, your family, and your loved ones. Things may be difficult for you right now, but just trust in my timing. A change in your circumstances is coming." I couldn't believe that happened to be the message that came on that specific day. It was what I needed to hear. I immediately smiled and knew I was meant to read it at that exact moment.

Whenever you are in a place of despair, remember this: God is bigger than the giants you face.

He can conquer them and help you through it. All He asks of you is to trust Him and have faith in Him. We can do all things through Christ who strengthens us; we just have to let Him work in our hearts and our lives. He will show up for you when you least expect it: when the odds seem more against you than ever and when the obstacle looks too big. God will turn it around simply out of the goodness of who He is. Remain faithful in that; sometimes, all you have is your faith.

The next day, after the surgery, we head to Miami for a Cuban sandwich and an ultrasound checkup, just as we did after the first surgery. As we were in the room, I was holding my breath and restless to hear the update on the surgery. After knowing the first surgery didn't work, I was worried that we would have the same result this time, but shortly after he started to look at the ultrasound, Dr. Quintero told us good news. He said that the fluid decreased, and her right lung expanded to her diaphragm. This was a miracle, a true relief. This was what we needed to happen. I knew we were not done fighting, but we were taking small steps one day at a time, and it seemed to be working. One of the concerns he had was that Lily's lung had given up by this point, but that was not what was happening as her lung seemed to be bouncing back. He looks at the ultrasound and told us if the surgery happened to be planned for that day, it would have been impossible. She was not in a good position. It wasn't a coincidence that she just happened to be in a perfect position when it mattered the most. It was God working one of His many miracles.

We left that day feeling thankful and hopeful. Now would be the hardest part, the waiting game. We had to wait and see what would happen – if the shunts stayed in, if the lungs grew, and if she continued to develop normally. Some days, time felt like it was racing, like a movie where you have to rewind to remember what just happened. And others felt like slow motion. In the weekly visits to come, both shunts remained where they were supposed to be, and the fluid kept draining. We still had to be monitored every week just in case there was a change. Lily kept growing, but we were never technically "in the clear." I was a high-risk pregnancy and had to take it easy the rest of the way. I had to miss Taylor's, one of my best friend's wedding, where I was supposed to be her bridesmaid. Taylor and I dreamt of being in each other's weddings since we met; she was my bridesmaid just a few months prior. I also missed two other close friends' weddings. Those moments were devastating for me, but by Dr. Quintero's direction, we could not risk being far from him and the facility if something were to happen.

Now that Lily had the means to fight, we had to give her time to grow. There was still some fluid that needed to get out of her right lung, but now, more than ever, time was of the essence. Another surgery wasn't an option at this point; there was no more room in her chest cavity to place another shunt.

As the weeks went on, it still felt like a blur. I constantly had to ask myself what had happened.

I dreamt of the place we were in at this point. God knew this was what our journey would be from the day Dakota and I were born. How crazy. It felt impossible to overcome but here we were. Through God's grace and faithfulness, we were inching closer each day to meeting our baby. We still weren't sure what life would look like for her, but we at least hoped we would be able to meet her.

During a church service, I remember hearing, "you may see the float, but God sees the whole parade." This resonated with me because most times, I was only focusing on the exact moment we were in, but God could see the entire situation. He knew our outcome even when we were in the unknown. Not being in control throughout our journey was almost as hard as not knowing what the future held. We had to learn to surrender our hearts and minds to whatever His plan was. I quickly realized that sometimes, uncertainty forces us to pray like everything depends on God, and I was surely dependent on Him now.

Chapter 12

The Hope

Three months after the initial diagnosis, it was now January 2022, and Lily's right lung seemed to be growing and expanding exactly how it needed to be, and the fluid that was left seemed to be slowly draining. At one of the weekly appointments, we saw her practicing breathing on the ultrasound; it was incredible. We felt like we had helped her, and I kept praying and thanking God for our miracle baby. We prayed every night for Lily to have the strength to keep fighting and not give up; it seemed like our prayers were working. The fight still wasn't over, and it felt risky to enjoy the pregnancy, but each week we went to Dr. Quintero and Dr. Kontopoulos, it felt like we were getting closer to defying the odds and meeting our little girl. Our miracle.

The weekly appointments to Miami began to become our new routine. I would count down the days each week to Wednesday, as that was when we would get to see Lily. Dakota and I were truly living in a week-to-week mindset. Everything in our lives revolved around these appointments and our situation. Dr. Quintero began using words like "fantastic" and saying things look "unbelievable." I never thought I would hear him use those words when describing her status. Lily's right lung was now "essentially average," and she was measuring normal for her age. He said Lily could most likely use her lungs to breathe had she been born now, and I felt a bit of relief, but I knew we weren't done fighting yet. My due date was not for another two months.

We felt at peace with how things were going. I clung to my faith more than ever and prayed harder than I had in my whole life. I thanked God for our baby and often prayed a vivid prayer of laying Lily at His feet and giving her to Him for healing and protecting her, and He would pick her up and hold her in His arms. I prayed that He would give Dakota and I the strength to get through this journey, but more importantly, I prayed that He gave Lily the strength to keep fighting.

I remember at one of our appointments, we began talking about birth, and I was emotional as I did not think this was in the cards for us a few months ago. They told us that Lily would go to the NICU (Neonatal Intensive Care Unit) when she was born to make sure she could breathe, and ensure no air gets inside her chest cavity. She would have had a chest tube if that had happened. This thought made me feel uneasy; I wanted to have the birth other moms had, where they get to hold their baby after they make their grand appearance. I told myself it would be best for Lily to be in the care of the doctors since we didn't know what was to come when she was born.

We didn't have a middle name picked out for her yet, and we went back and forth on a few, but we knew it had to be something special. After thinking about our journey and debating ideas, it came to us: Lily Faith. It was clear that this had to be her name. Faith means that you have peace even when you don't have all the answers. And Hebrews 11:1 says that Faith is confidence in what we hope for and assurance about what we do not see.

Lily brought faith to us and everyone around us. All those who were on this journey with us had grown their faith, and it was because of our baby that our own faith grew stronger. Dakota and I started praying together and even some family members who were not big believers were the ones setting up prayer circles every week to pray for us. Lily was so strong and such a fighter; she never once gave up, even when the odds were stacked against her in more than one situation. All I could think about was how I would, hopefully, one day, be able to share our journey with her and explain the reason her middle name is Faith. I knew the fight wasn't over; I knew that we still had to trust God's plan and hope things kept going smoothly but as the weeks went on, it felt more and more like our story was going to have a happy ending.

At times it was hard to be happy and excited. I mean, after all, the doctors initially told us our baby wasn't going to make it, and if she did, she would need life-long care. My heart would ache whenever I thought about the day we got the news and I kept trying to focus on the positives but would break down most days. All I ever wanted in life was to be a mom; I dreamt of these days and moments, but I had to keep going. Lily needed me to be strong. She could feel my energy and feed off my feelings; I had to remain calm for her. She needed me. There were moments that were tougher than others, but no matter what we were faced with, we chose faith. Not once in the Bible does it say to worry about it, stress over it, or lose sleep because of it. But God does tell us to trust in His plan over and over again, even when we don't understand. And we did not understand why this was our journey, but we had to continue to have hope.

Chapter 13

The Seed

The next two weeks, we received great news. Lily's right lung was fulling, expanding, and hugging her heart. It was right up against her diaphragm like it needed to be. Dr. Quintero could barely see the fluid around her lung at this point. She was measuring average for her age, and all her organs were receiving blood flow and oxygen; this was a reassuring sign.

Both of Lily's shunts stayed in place, and things were on track. We got to a point where Dr. Quintero was alluding to the fact that he thought Lily would make it; it was never definite, but it seemed to be turning more positive. Dr. Quintero told us there was fluid left in Lily's right lung, but it was "inconsequential, very minor, and nothing to worry about." He measured the fluid that was left in her lung, and it was .3mm. I took a small gasp of air when he told me this. The amount of fluid in her lung is the same size as a mustard seed. I smiled when I realized this. I couldn't believe it. Sometimes God has a funny way of showing you that He is there, and the closer you are to God, the more often you see Him working in mysterious and wonderfully incredible ways. And this was one of those moments. I knew once again that God had our situation and Lily's under control. I wholeheartedly knew it.

I was still holding onto a thread of excitement, not letting myself be happy yet. I knew anything could happen, but I continued to trust God and give it all to Him. I couldn't carry this alone, nor did I want to try. It was too much to bear. We had come so far. All Dakota and I had were each other. We kept reminding ourselves that God didn't bring us this far to only bring us this far. He wasn't going to bring us through this tribulation for there to not be a reason or purpose. There was a purpose for the pain, the worry, and the fear. He was going to save her and bring her here healthy. We believed that. We had to.

It was a Saturday morning in February, and it was my baby shower. I had mixed emotions about this day as I was told a few short months before that it was not an option for us. Our friends and family came, prayed over me and Lily, celebrated how far we had come, and reconfirmed the community of support that was formed around Dakota and me. As I began to speak and thank everyone for attending, my heart burst with joy and reflection. I could not get through my speech without pausing through the emotions.

After all, these were the people that loved us and prayed on their knees for us and for Lily. I owed them everything. They will never understand the amount of gratitude I felt on this day. The power of prayer is real; I felt it in that moment. Lily's journey is evident in this. God knew the outcome of our story before we even knew what was going to happen. Praise God for our community, and thank You, God, for ours.

Two days after my baby shower, I was 37 weeks and as sick as could be. After not being able to keep water down for three hours, Dakota took me to the ER. Dehydration when pregnant is not something you want, especially in my circumstance. I ended up with norovirus. After having an IV of fluids, my heart rate and Lily's became more stable. I remained faithful in prayer and petition and knew this was another challenge we had to overcome. Just when we thought we are in the clear, something else came up. But I had faith. My main worry was that Lily would get the virus and not be able to fight it, but Dr. Quintero said she would be okay. The day after I was better, Dakota caught the virus. I had to call 9-1-1 as he could not walk due to being so weak. It was scary, and we were entering the unknown again. I kept praying and asking God to heal him in time for Lily to be here, as at this point, it could be any day now. Thankfully, after a day in the hospital, he was home.

Even when the odds were stacked against us, we stayed faithful. The devil does not attack strong walls, he attacks when we are weak, and we cannot allow those opportunities to present themselves. God tells us that He will make a way when there seems to be no way. We just must trust and have hope in Him and Him alone. I clung to this truth throughout the pregnancy, even before we got the initial news. Isaiah 40:31 says that, "Those that trust in the Lord will find new strength," and we sure had to find that.

Chapter 14

The Angel's Kiss

February 15th was our last appointment in Miami. Lily was practicing breathing on the ultrasound, and I was scheduled to be induced on February 22nd with Dr. Quintero and Dr. Kontopoulos. I didn't want to risk not having them deliver Lily. I wanted the same doctors that placed the shunts into her to be the ones to remove them. We made the arrangements, and when I got home from the appointment, I had the hospital bags packed and was mentally prepared to be in the NICU for weeks. I could not believe we were at this point.

It was the evening of February 16th, and we received a terrible news: Dakota's grandpa had passed away. It took us all by surprise and was tough to accept. We were so upset about the loss of such a wonderful man, especially because all he wanted to do was to meet Lily. Rozz and her dad were very close, and it broke our hearts to see her so shattered.

Dakota is the first grandchild of that side of his family, and the emptiness that filled our hearts after the loss was deep. We found out that he ended up having fluid in his lungs, just like Lily did, but he wasn't strong enough to heal from that, amongst other things. We all knew deep down that Papa is Lily's guardian angel.

February 20th, we were thrilled and worried at the same time but kept praying as we had no idea what to expect. The next day, we were planning to go to Miami and stay at a hotel near the hospital so we wouldn't have to make the long drive on the day of the induction. We couldn't help but think about how this journey was a long-fought battle and how God gave His hardest battles to His strongest soldiers. That is what I want to be—God's soldier. You are required to be a soldier when you're at the forefront of a battle with the devil, and all the odds are stacked against you. But with God on your side, nothing is impossible.

Before going to sleep, we quickly realized that Lily had other plans. Around 9:30 p.m., my water broke, but I was convinced that it was not. It took some persuading from Dakota and Rozz, and then the rest of my water breaking, like a movie scene, for me to realize what was happening. I was ready but concerned. I just wanted her to be okay. I just wanted her to survive and be healthy. We had no idea what was going to happen and a flood of questions came to my mind. How long would she be in the NICU?

Would she be taken away from us right when she was born for tests? Would she come out breathing? Would she be immediately placed in emergency surgery? The questions didn't end, but I had to focus. I had to make sure I did all I could to get her here safely.

We called Taina and she said we should head to the hospital that was closer to us instead of all the way in Miami and that was what we did. We headed to Wellington, about 30 minutes away. We called our families to tell them the situation and they were ecstatic yet unsure of the outcome. We arrived at the hospital, and the maternity ward was closed, so we went through the ER. It was packed for a Sunday night. Dakota had to bring the bags in as I got admitted. By the time he got to the room, I had my IV in, and Dr. Quintero was on his way.

At this point, Lily was carefully and closely monitored. She had more doctors assigned to her than any other baby on the maternity floor. We were assigned one of the kindest nurses I had ever met, Ann. She was tending to our every need and I had hoped it was because that was her job and not because she wasn't sure how our baby would turn out. She was caring and cautious about how I was doing emotionally. It was time for the epidural, and Dakota left the room. I looked at Ann and said, "Do you believe in God?" And she smiled and said, "Yes, I do." I said, "Can I pray with you while I get the epidural?" And she said, "Of course!" Only Ann and I were in the room with the man who was doing the epidural. I was so scared. I began to pray out loud as she held me still for the needle to go in. I asked God for protection over Lily and to bring her into the world safely and healthy; I prayed for Dr. Quintero as he would be delivering for us, I prayed for strength to get through whatever was coming our way, and I prayed that He would be with us every step. It wasn't long after the epidural that it was time. Dr. Quintero was there and Ann was by my side. We heard a knock at the door and Val came in. I was so happy to see her. It felt like a full circle. The first nurse to see us for the first surgery was now in the room to see our miracle baby be born. It was a special moment having her there.

After 30 minutes of pushing, Lily came out screaming...I could not believe it. Did her lungs work? Is this truly happening? It felt like life just paused for a split second and then I heard another cry. Her lungs worked! I was overwhelmed with joy. Praise God! Lily was born February 21st, weighing 6 pounds 9 ounces, and was 18.5 inches long. I felt so relieved. I was an emotional wreck. My baby was here. She was okay. Dr. Quintero removed the two shunts from her body and showed them to us; they were much larger than we thought. He put bandages over the holes in her back where the shunts were placed. I was worried air would go in and she would have to have a chest tube, but he indicated she was okay and that her holes would close. Dakota was standing with Lily while they did all the routine tests. Then they placed her on me, and I had never felt that feeling before. Love, relief, strength, and joy were all bundled up in one thing. WHAT A MIRACLE! I worked so hard for her. Dakota and I both did. We never let go of our faith, even when it would've been so much easier to give up. Not once. I felt a wave of relief and a weight lift off my shoulder. This day felt so far away for us for so long and here we were.

Papa passed away only five days before Lily was born. Looking back, I think that he had to go to heaven for her to be here. She came out with an angel's kiss on her forehead, and we like to think that it was from Papa. Ten or so minutes went by, and Dakota went to the NICU with Lily while I recovered then got wheel-chaired to her. Her cry was the most amazing sound I had ever heard. It proved her lungs were working. The feeling of holding her was breathtaking. I have never felt that amount of love or feeling of protection. I would do anything for her. I never wanted to put her down; I could've held her forever.

Chapter 15

The Scan

While I was recovering, Dakota texted me that Lily was about to get an x-ray to see how her lungs were. I was immediately nervous but knew she was in the right place. I was praying it would come back okay. I couldn't imagine something being wrong with her after all we had done to get to this point. Five minutes later, Dakota texted me and said, "It came back normal!" I cried with happiness alone in the delivery room. Her lungs were normal! She was okay and I was speechless.

Lily was in the NICU for 24 hours, where she was monitored for heart rate and oxygen levels. I could not stop staring at the screen to make sure the numbers did not drop. I couldn't believe she was breathing on her own. God is so good. Dr. Quintero and Dr. Kontopoulos saved her life. At this point, Dakota and I would be with her most of the time, then would come back throughout the night so I could feed her.

I hated leaving her in the NICU all alone. She needed her mom. But I knew this was best.

Later that day, we were in the postpartum room and there was a knock on the door. It was Ann! I was so glad to see her. I didn't know if I would ever see her again. She came in carrying a basket full of goodies for Lily and us. Champagne, baby socks and shoes, an outfit for Lily, and a book. I looked at the book, and it was titled "Baby's First Bible." I was so emotional; I hugged her. It was such a special moment I will never forget. She began to explain to Dakota and me that on her way to work the day before, she was having a rough time and prayed and asked God for a sign that she could continue going through whatever battle it was. Ann looked at us and said, "You were my sign; Lily was my sign. She is a miracle." By now, all three of us were crying and were in complete and utter awe at the miracle baby that had just entered our world and changed not only our lives but those around her. This baby was inspiring so many people and she wasn't even a day old.

On February 22nd, Lily had to get an x-ray before being discharged to the postpartum room with us. I was anxious. I had to step away because I feared what it would show. But then, I remembered I was a soldier of God. I could do anything with Him in my corner. I began to pray. I was worried they would see something wrong with her and the fluid would return. I thought I loved her when she was in my belly, but having her earthside showed me a whole new level of love I didn't know existed. I couldn't lose her now that I have her. She's my baby, a part of me. I would do anything for her. The x-ray was quick, and the doctor looked at us and said everything looked normal.

Relief overwhelmed us and we teared up and stared at Lily laying in the NICU bed. I knew for a fact; at that moment, she was a true miracle—just like all the miracles you read in the Bible. I couldn't believe it. But then again, I could. I knew God had her in His protection and behind His shield this whole time. It was just hard sometimes to see in the low moments, but I believed it all along. I prayed that God would take Lily under His wings and give her all she needed. Our prayers changed throughout our journey, but we were specific with our prayers and made sure to thank Him for the ability to have a chance. It felt like we finally had made it. We had come so far. We were going to bring our girl home, just like Dakota told me we would.

Mark 10:27 in the Bible says that "with man, this is impossible, but not with God; all things are possible with God." We are a living testimony of His faithfulness to this. In 1 Chronicles 16:34, it says, "Give thanks to the Lord for He is good; His love endures forever." For one of the first times in my life, I personally saw this come to fruition. Through our repetitiveness of prayer, and praises towards Him throughout our journey, we stayed strong and steadfast in His name. He is good, and His love for us and Lily is proof of that. Miracles can happen and we praise God for ours.

A Mustard Seed of Faith

Chapter 16

The Drive

Lily came with us to the postpartum room, and we were speechless. We were so in love with our miracle baby. It was a dream. Our prayers were answered above and beyond. Lily was perfectly HEALTHY. Like nothing ever happened. WHAT?! How is this even possible? I barely slept. Maybe it was the nurses constantly checking in, but it felt like it was because we had our beautiful miracle sleeping next to us; I was in complete shock.

The next morning Lily had a few standard tests done and was released, meaning there was no need for her to stay at the hospital. I was slightly embarrassed at the amount I had packed because we thought we would be in the NICU for weeks. When Dr. Quintero video called us to discharge me, Dakota held up Lily to the computer camera. I saw the biggest smile on Dr. Quintero's face. This was the baby he saved. The life he saved. He was a hero. We were so thankful for the medical advancements that we experienced and the amazing doctors who had so much compassion and motivation to save lives. After a few laughs and smiles, some tears, and a ton of "thank yous," I was discharged.

It was now late afternoon on February 23rd, and we were headed home. Even though we had no idea how to raise a child, this was a dream come true. As we were driving home, with Lily in her car seat, I completely broke down. I will never forget this feeling. Crying for no other reason but relief, happiness, and gratitude to God. All my emotions came at once, like a tidal wave. Dr. Seena told us Lily wouldn't make it, yet here she was. She said Lily would need lifelong care, yet here she was, breathing normal and perfectly healthy. Dr. Desnet said it's likely she would pass away in utero, yet here she was. Lily defied the odds. She was and still is a miracle. She was not supposed to be here, yet here we are. Dakota told me if it wasn't genetic, we were going to bring our girl home, and that was what we did.

Throughout the pregnancy, I would tell my mom that I wouldn't be happy or feel completely at ease until we left the hospital with Lily. That was when it finally hit me that she was okay. Our dream came true. The day we had prayed for and hoped for was finally here. Our girl was healthy. We were finally a family of three. We still couldn't believe she was here and breathing on her own. Bringing her home was the best day of our lives.

In Isaiah 43:2, God says, "when you go through deep waters, I will be with you." It truly felt like, in that moment, God was lifting us out of the deep waters we were in. We made it. He had carried us through. Lily was here, healthy, has no lasting issues, no specialists, no routine checkups, absolutely nothing! It felt like we had run the longest marathon of our life, and we had just crossed the finish line and laid on the ground, panting with relief. It was the biggest fight of our lives, and I thank God He brought us through it.

When you feel like you are at a point in your life where you can't see a light at the end of your tunnel, stay faithful to Him. Trust that he will carry you through that deep water. God says in Jeremiah 29:11, "For I know the plans I have for you," declares the Lord, "plans to prosper you and not to harm you, plans to give you hope and a future." Trust that His plan is carefully crafted for you out of love and sincerity. In moments when you have nothing else, cling to your faith and see the miracles that you begin to encounter and the coincidences that seem more like "signs." Lily is a living testimony of His goodness and love for us. Her journey happened for a reason, and she was made to do wonderful things for the kingdom of God.

Chapter 17

The Heroes

I n April 2022, we went to Dr. Quintero and Dr.
Kontopoulous for our 6-week checkup. It was
emotional for us as we had made this same
drive to Miami while I was pregnant so frequently.
We arrived at The Fetal Institute and it was surreal
walking into the same doors and office that we
had when we were in such a state of the unknown.
I couldn't help but hold back the tears when the
doctors came and saw Lily. They saw and held the
baby they saved. I could only imagine how rewarding
this felt for them. They felt like family after we had
spent so much time together, and I struggled to
get any words out about how grateful I was for their
efforts.

As they held Lily, I pulled out a canvas that was
hiding and presented them with it. It was a photo of
Lily that said:

Fetal Hydrops and two Thoracoamniotic Shunt Placement Survivor.

Thank you, Dr. Q and Dr. K, for saving my life.

It was a picture-perfect moment. I also gave them a thank-you card which felt silly because how can you properly thank someone who legitimately saved your child? I knew that day was just as special for them as it was for us. The canvas of Lily now hangs in their office space, with all the other canvases of babies that they have saved. I dreamt of this moment since the first day we came to their office, and I saw all the babies on the wall. We had made it to our happy ending.

A few months later, in June 2022, we went to Dr. Ivy for our 6-month appointment with Lily. This was the same doctor that helped us get the appointment with Dr. Desnet, the fetal cardiologist. She was Dakota's pediatrician, and of course, she had to be Lily's. She examined Lily as she had a cold, and Dr. Ivy suggested we get an ultrasound and x-ray of her lungs just to make sure everything was okay. My mom came with me and we went to the hospital the next day. Of course, I did not sleep much the night before. I was nervous that something was wrong with her again and that we would get bad news. It had been a wonderful six months; I couldn't imagine something happening now. I thought we already went through enough. Lily was perfect and smiling during the scans, and the doctor said the ultrasound looked good. We wouldn't have the x-ray results for another day or so. I was relieved to hear the ultrasound was good; I said, "I'll take it!"

Dakota and I were in the kitchen when we received a call from Dr. Ivy the next day. She said that the x-ray looked normal. Dakota and I hugged, and it truly felt like we had made it. Another clear scan and x-ray, what a miracle. We felt like we were on cloud nine.

Not all endings end up the way ours did. Sometimes, that is the hardest thing to accept – God's plan over your own. Trust that things happen for a reason and that there is something to get out of it. Stop asking God to get you out of a bad situation but rather ask Him what it is that you should get out of it. You may come to find that things ended up better than you may have expected. Sometimes unanswered prayers are just what you need, even when you can't see why.

Chapter 18

The Army

A year after Lily's diagnosis, in October 2022, it all started to make sense. It felt like this was what God's plan was for us. It took me months to feel grateful for the journey. Grateful for the hard days when we got bad news at appointments, sleepless nights full of research and tears, the worry and fear. But God wanted us to go through this. He wanted Lily to be here, she was meant to be here, and He made it happen. There were days when I questioned why we had to go through what we did. Why us? But then it hit me and I realized that if the only reason we went through what we did was to get others to be closer to Jesus and for their faith to be strengthened, then it was worth it. Maybe God assigned us this mountain to show others it could be moved. And maybe God allowed the odds to be stacked against us so He could reveal more of His glory in our lives.

1 Peter 5:10 says, "And the God of all grace, who called you to His eternal glory in Christ, after you have suffered a little while, will Himself restore you and make you strong, firm and steadfast." Maybe we had to go through our trial to allow Him to restore us and make us stronger than we were before. Looking back, I can now say, staring at my healthy eight-month-old, that it was worth it. Although the battle belongs to Him, God continuously seeks out His army, and Lily leads the pack.

Chapter 19

The Connection

One night, I was reflecting on where we were one year ago. I was on bed rest from one surgery and about to have another. As I stared at Lily, it felt like a lifetime ago that we were in one of the hardest situations of our lives. I began to get emotional as Lily was laying on me, and I knew there was something I wanted to do. I searched the Brianna Marie Foundation, the one that Dr. Quintero had told me about. I called the number online and left a message for Aran, the mom of Brianna Marie, the baby that passed away from the same condition Lily survived. She called me back a few minutes later, and we immediately connected. There is nothing like two moms who went through the same thing connecting on a level that no one else can understand.

We began talking, and we told each other about the journeys we both went through. We talk about

God and faith and how that was what carried us through. Unfortunately, Brianna Marie passed away as her lungs didn't have enough time to grow after all the shunt surgeries Aran had. God had other plans for them. They created the Foundation in Brianna Marie's honor and all the other babies that became angels too soon. Aran's mission with the foundation is to help other physicians and families learn about the benefits of fetal therapies and the life-saving surgeries that can be performed prior to a child's birth. They raise money for fetal therapy, which goes back to the research of our doctors, Dr. Quintero and Dr. Kontopoulos. These doctors are doing remarkable things for families all around the world. They saved Lily and attempted all they could for Brianna.

Aran and Patrick were sent to Dr. Quintero and Dr. Kontopoulos too late in their pregnancy for there to be anything to do. We resonated with each other on the phone, we laughed, we cried, and I asked how I could help with the Foundation. Aran offered for me to do the opening prayer at the 2023 5K race, where all the children that were saved by Dr. Quintero and Dr. Kontopoulos come with their families to give thanks and celebrate. It was one of the biggest honors I had ever been asked.

As we were wrapping up our call, Aran paused and said, "If you want to talk about signs from God, I have one for you." I was curious and quiet. She proceeded to say, "My birthday is February 21st as well." My eyes swelled up, and I couldn't believe it. The woman whose life mission is to help babies conquer what her daughter couldn't, has the same birthday as my baby, who survived the diagnosis. The Brianna Marie Foundation raises money for the doctors that saved Lily to be able to have more opportunities for research to help save more lives. And the woman behind it all was Aran, who shared Lily's birthday. It was a beautiful moment that I will always remember.

Chapter 20

The Spirit

I t is now February 2023, and Lily is the happiest, most joyous baby I have ever seen. Not to mention she is healthy! She lights up the room and her smile is contagious. Her first birthday is in a few weeks, and most days, I cannot wrap my head around the fact that we are here. We are so grateful. She is our miracle baby, and we love her beyond measure. My four Bible study prayer warriors and I have weekly play dates with the girls, and Lily loves giving hugs and waving to everyone. She is a bit too friendly with strangers and hugged the waiter at the restaurant the other day. She loves our dog, Tucker, and blows him kisses. She says "dada" all day and "mama" when she is crying, but hey, I'll take it. She has a personality that is so vibrant and radiates joy and love. She is curious, smart, and loves music and animals, especially birds. I know that the Holy Spirit is shining through her and in her.

She is the sweetest baby and a tough, sometimes stubborn cookie too. We are so blessed, and I thank God every day for her.

The Bible says in 1 Corinthians 2:9, "No eye has seen, no ear has heard, and no mind has imagined the things that God has prepared for those who love him." God has our greater good in mind and He is restoring all things in us through His love. Do not lose faith in God because when He says a thing, He will surely bring it to pass. I hope that God allowed Dakota, Lily, and I to pass through our battle so that others could believe in Him and be reminded that there's nothing impossible for Him to do.

Chapter 21

The Miracle

R eflecting back, there were many things that happened during our journey that others would see as coincidences, but I knew God had His hand on us. I prayed harder than I ever had during these times. God heard my prayers. He answered them. But all along, He knew this was going to happen. He knew what we would go through before we were even married. It was a part of our story and Lily's story. She survived for a reason. She has a purpose. We had to trust Him and completely let Him be in control; the situation was out of our hands. It didn't happen right away, but I had to let faith take over and keep praying; there was no other choice but to do so.

Let Lily's testimony and our story inspire you to keep fighting when faced with difficulties. Know that things happen for a reason and that there is hope in the unknown. When the odds were against us in more ways than one, we kept pushing through and did not give up. We did not let the negativity sneak in, although it tried to on more than one occasion. I hope this story helps you if you are struggling to get through a tough time and do not see the light at the end of your tunnel. Stay strong, give it to God, keep the faith, and don't lose hope. The devil wouldn't be attacking you so hard if there wasn't something Holy inside of you. Sometimes, you just need to be reminded that God's plan is better. This is your reminder. He is working for your good.

Situations can change in the blink of an eye, and life is short. We were close to not meeting our baby, and now, she is flourishing and perfectly healthy. We trusted God and He showed up for us. Know that He can and will do the same for you. Give it to Him. Be a soldier of God; prove to others that you can move your mountains too.

I pray that you are graced with the strength and perseverance to continue fighting your battle, big or small. I pray that Lily's testimony and our story bring you hope in the dark times and prove to you that there is something to put your faith in. Not everyone has a happy ending to their fight but trust that there is a bigger and better purpose and plan for you than you could ever think of on your own. You may not see it now, but one day, you will.

Lily is such a fighter and is so strong. She is beautiful inside and out and lights up every room she is in. When all the odds were against her, she fought, and we fought. She didn't give up, and neither did we. She inspires us every day. Lily is going to change more lives than she already has, and I pray she continues to shine her light on others. She is our miracle baby, and we are blessed. Looking back, I can confidently say a .3mm mustard seed of faith was all it took to move our mountain.

Acknowledgements

Lily, you are my joy. We prayed for you and fought so hard for you. You are the sweetest little girl, and I am blessed to be your mommy. I pray that the Holy Spirit works in and through you. Continue to shine, sweet girl; you were made to do wonderful things. I love you forever.

Dakota, words could never describe how thankful I am that I have you by my side. You are my rock, my strength, my person. I love you and thank God you are mine. You are my better half, and I couldn't have conquered this journey without you. No one else will ever understand what we went through; I am thankful to have had each other. Lily has no idea how lucky she is to have you as her daddy.

Mom and Dad, thank you for giving me the gift of life. I never knew how much you loved me until I had a baby of my own, and then it made sense. Thank you for loving Lily and praying for her, your first grand baby. Mom, thank you for always being there; you are the one I can count on. You were right all along.

Dad, you are my best friend, and I am forever blessed to be your daughter; I love you. Thank you for all you do.

Rozz, thank you for being my prayer warrior, helping me on some of the hardest days, and being by my side through it all. You are the best mother-in-law I could've asked for.

Devon, thank you for always supporting us, never giving up on us, and loving Lily so well. You and Rozz showed up for us in more ways than one and we couldn't have gotten through this without either of you.

Ben, you are my partner in crime; no one gets me like you do. I love you. Thank you for standing by our side and praying for us throughout the entire journey. Lily is lucky to have you.

Ali, thank you for supporting Ben, being there for not only him, but for us, and praying for us. You are the best sister and aunt to Lily I could've asked for to join our family.

Austin and Kolton, no one else gets you like your siblings. You two were there for us, prayed for us, and your niece is so lucky to have you to protect her and love her through life. I am so thankful to call you my brothers. I love you both tremendously.

A Mustard Seed of Faith

My girls, you know who you are. You got me through the worst moments of my life and diligently prayed for us. My life is better with you in it, and I can't wait to raise our babies together.

Dr. Quintero and Dr. Kontopoulos, thank you for saving our baby. There are no words to thank you enough. I know God had a plan for you both to be a part of our journey. Thank you for being the only ones to give us hope. You are our heroes.

To everyone who prayed for us, whether you know us personally or not, thank you.

If you or someone you know if faced with a negative fetal diagnosis, please consider contacting www.the-fetal-institute.com to discuss your options with a medical professional.